SHORT WAL

MADE EASY

NORTHUMBERLAND

Contents

Distance
2.4 miles/3.9km

GO BY TRAIN

Time
1¼ hours

Start/Finish
Berwick-upon-Tweed

Parking TD15 1NE
Greens Haven car park by Magdalene Fields

Cafés/pubs
Berwick-upon-Tweed

Historic town walls walk and clifftop sea views

Berwick Barracks

Page 14

Walk 5

ALNWICK

Distance
3.5 miles/5.6km

Time
1¾ hours

CATCH A BUS

Start/Finish
Alnwick

Parking NE66 1SF
Greenwell Road
car park

Cafés/pubs
Alnwick

Scenic parkland and riverside stroll; view of magnificent castle

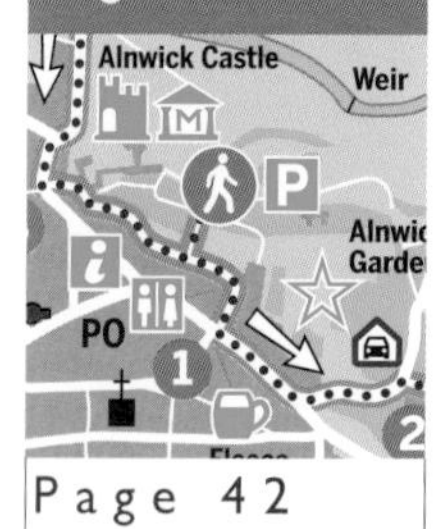

Page 42

Walk 6

WARKWORTH

Distance
2.9 miles/4.7km

Time
1½ hours

CATCH A BUS

Start/Finish
Warkworth

Parking NE65 0SW
Warkworth Beach
car park

Cafés/pubs
Warkworth

Looping riverside, striking hilltop castle and historic bridge

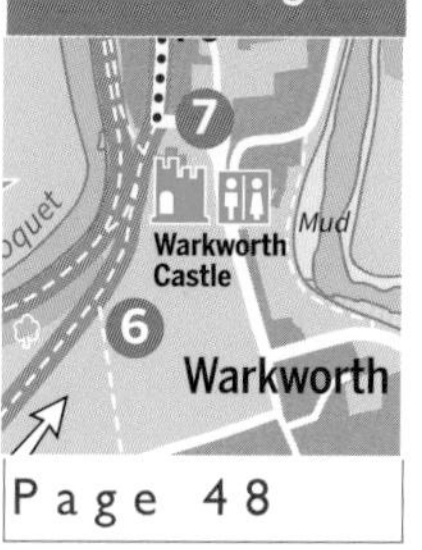

Page 48

Walk 7

KIELDER WATER

Distance
4 miles/6.4km

Time
2 hours

Start/Finish
Kielder Water

Parking NE48 1BH
Hawkhope car park,
Falstone

Cafés/pubs
In nearby Falstone

Expansive lake, monumental forest, osprey and red squirrel

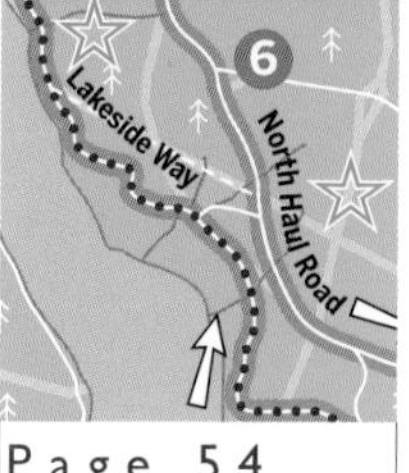

Page 54

Walk 8

SHAFTOE CRAGS

Distance
4.8 miles/7.7km

Time
2½ hours

Start/Finish
Bowlam Lake

Parking NE20 0HG
West Wood car park, Scot's Gap road

Cafés/pubs
Bowlam Lake Coutry Park visitor centre

Fabulous weather-sculpted rocks, lovely lake and woodlands

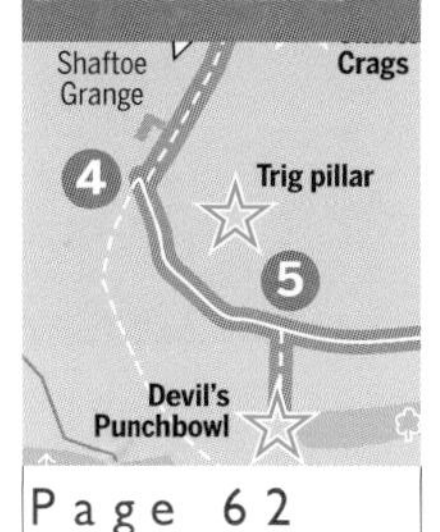

Walk 9

HADRIAN'S WALL

Distance
2.6 miles/4.2km

Time
1¾ hours

CATCH A BUS (the AD122)

Start/Finish
Cawfields Quarry

Parking NE49 9NN
Cawfields Quarry car park

Cafés/pubs
In nearby Haltwhistle

World Heritage Site wall and milecastle; Pennine views

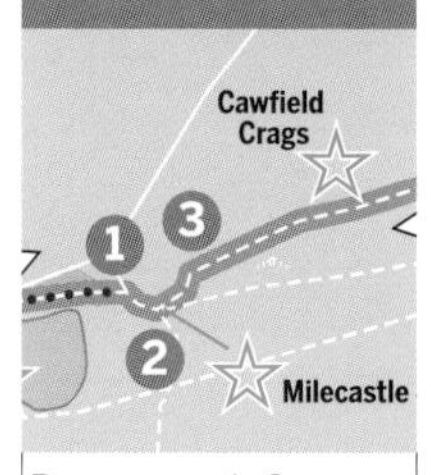

Walk 10

RIVER TYNE AT HEXHAM

Distance
3.5 miles/5.6km

Time
1¾ hours

GO BY TRAIN CATCH A BUS

Start/Finish
Hexham

Parking NE46 3HQ
Tyne Green Country Park car park

Cafés/pubs
Café Enna, Tynedale Golf Club

Combined town, riverside and parkland trails full of interest

GETTING OUTSIDE IN NORTHUMBERLAND

“”

Northumberland National Park, where you can be mesmerized by starlight in England's first International Dark Sky Park

OS Champion
Dave Wilson

Hadrian's Wall

A very warm welcome to the new Short Walks Made Easy guide to Northumberland – what a fantastic selection of leisurely walks we have for you!

There is so much to explore and enjoy throughout Northumberland, England's most northerly county and sixth largest by area: from the stunning beach and bracing North Sea backdrop at Bamburgh Castle, part of the North Northumberland Heritage Coast, to the epic spectacle of Hadrian's Wall – a World Heritage Site – at Cawfield Crags, and the expansive reservoir and extensive woodlands of Kielder Forest Park.

The Northumberland Coast, a designated Area of Outstanding Natural Beauty (AONB), is explored at its finest on our walk between the little fishing port of Craster and the iconic headland ruin of Dunstanburgh Castle. At Hexham, an ancient crossing point of the Tyne where we stroll beside the river, the North Pennines AONB stretches southwards. In between the two lies Northumberland National Park, where you can be mesmerized by starlight in England's first International Dark Sky Park.

Like no other, the Northumbrian landscape is infused with echoes of the past – often in troubled times, rooted in cross-border conflicts from the Roman age through to the 17th century – as can be witnessed on Hadrian's Wall, the town walls at Berwick-upon-Tweed, and the striking hilltop fortifications at Alnwick and Warkworth.

Coastal walks present the opportunity to spot seals and eider ducks. At Kielder you might be lucky enough to see an osprey or a red squirrel, while tranquil Wooler Common is a lovely place for a picnic and enjoying far-reaching views.

Dave Wilson, OS Champion

Kielder Water

Whether it's a short walk during our lunch break or a full day's outdoor adventure, we know that a good dose of fresh air is just the tonic we all need.

At Ordnance Survey (OS), we're passionate about helping more people to get outside more often. It sits at the heart of everything we do, and through our products and services, we aim to help you lead an active outdoor lifestyle, so that you can live longer, stay younger and enjoy life more.

We firmly believe the outdoors is for everyone, and we want to help you find the very best Great Britain has to offer. We are blessed with an island that is beautiful and unique, with a rich and varied landscape. There are coastal paths to meander along, woodlands to explore, countryside to roam, and cities to uncover. Our trusted source of inspirational content is bursting with ideas for places to go, things to do and easy beginner's guides on how to get started.

It can be daunting when you're new to something, so we want to bring you the know-how from the people who live and breathe the outdoors. To help guide us, our team of awe-inspiring OS Champions share their favourite places to visit, hints and tips for outdoor adventures, as well as tried and tested accessible, family and wheelchair-friendly routes. We hope that you will feel inspired to spend more time outside and reap the physical and mental health benefits that the outdoors has to offer. With our handy guides, paper and digital mapping, and exciting new apps, we can be with you every step of the way.

To find out more visit os.uk/getoutside

RESPECTING THE COUNTRYSIDE

You can't beat getting outside in the British countryside, but it's vital that we leave no trace when we're enjoying the great outdoors.

Let's make sure that generations to come can enjoy the countryside just as we do.

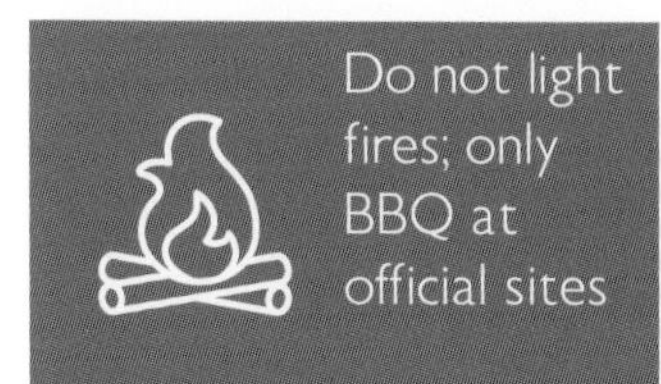

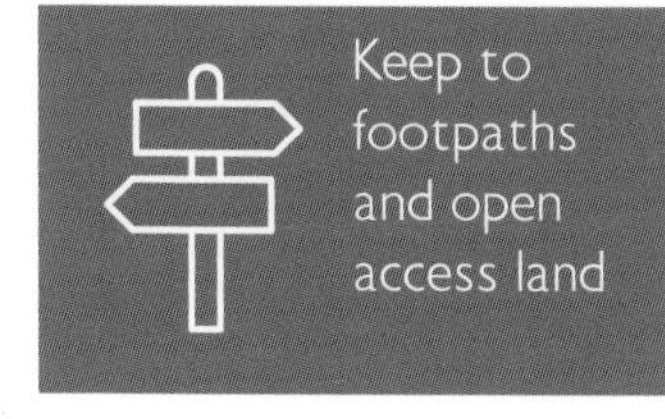

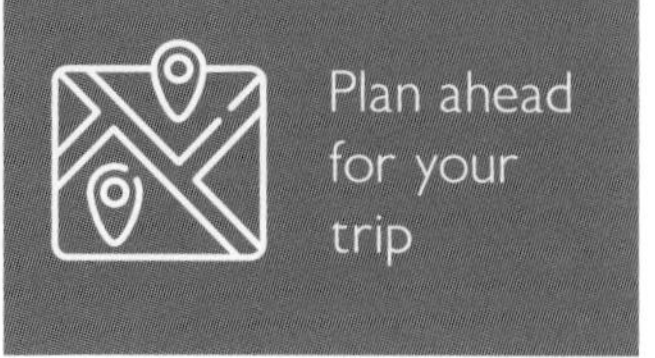

For more details please visit www.gov.uk/countryside-code

USING THIS GUIDE

Easy-to-follow Northumberland walks for all

Before setting off

Check the walk information panel to plan your outing

- Consider using **Public transport** where flagged. If driving, note the satnav postcode for the car park under **Parking**
- The suggested **Time** is based on a gentle pace
- Note the availability of **Cafés**, tearooms and pubs, and **Toilets**

Terrain and hilliness

- **Terrain** indicates the nature of the route surface
- Any rises and falls are noted under **Hilliness**

Walking with your dog?

- This panel states where **Dogs** *must* be on a lead and how many stiles there are – in case you need to lift your dog
- Keep dogs on leads where there are livestock and between April and August in forest where there are ground-nesting birds

A perfectly pocket-sized walking guide

- Handily sized for ease of use on each walk
- When not being read, it fits nicely into a pocket...
- ...so between points, put this book in the pocket of your coat, trousers or day sack and enjoy your stroll in glorious national park countryside – we've made it pocket-sized for a reason!

Flexibility of route presentation to suit all readers

- **Not comfortable map reading?** Then use the simple-to-follow route profile and accompanying route description and pictures
- **Happy to map read?** New-look walk mapping makes it easier for you to focus on the route and the points of interest along the way
- **Read the insightful Did you know?, Local legend, Stories behind the walk** and **Nature notes** to help you make the most of your day out and to enjoy all that each walk has to offer

The easy-to-use walk map

- **Large-scale** mapping for ultra-clear route finding
- **Numbered points** at key turns along the route that tie in with the route instructions and respective points marked on the profile
- **Pictorial symbols** for intuitive map reading, see Map Symbols on the front cover flap

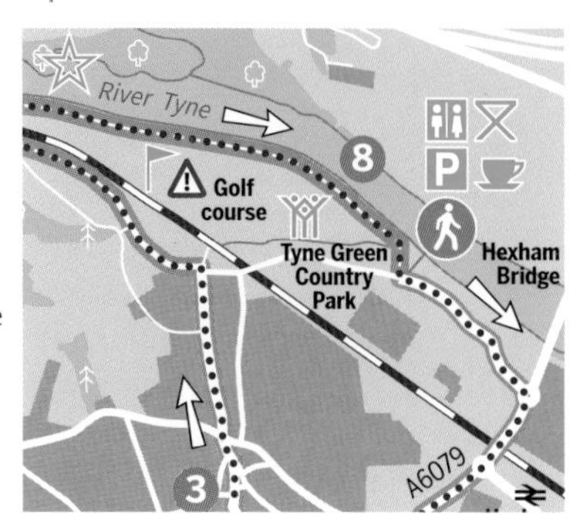

The simple-to-follow walk profile

- Progress easily along the route using the illustrative profile, it has **numbered points** for key turning points and **graduated distance** markers
- Easy-read **route directions** with turn-by-turn detail
- Reassuring **route photographs** for each numbered point

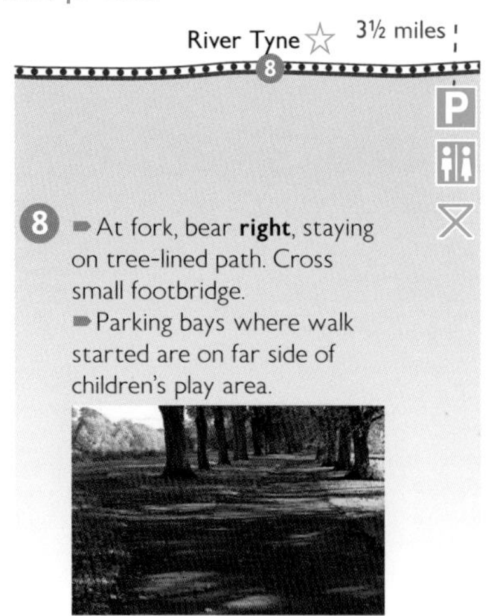

Many of the features and symbols shown are taken from Ordnance Survey's celebrated **Explorer** mapping, designed to help people across Great Britain enjoy leisure time spent outside. For more on this – and how you can start planning your own walks and adventures, please see the inside back cover.

WALK 1

BERWICK-UPON-TWEED

The bastioned walls around the border town of Berwick-upon-Tweed were built in the reign of Elizabeth I and still stand strong today. Surfaced paths enable walkers to stroll along the top of the defences, sometimes looking down on the attractive town within, sometimes looking along the River Tweed to the North Sea beyond. This figure-of-eight route combines the fascinating wall circuit, full of historic interest, with a short walk along the cliffs near the sandy bay of Fisherman's Haven.

Distance
2.4 miles/3.9km

Time
1¼ hours

Start/Finish
Berwick-upon-Tweed

Parking TD15 1NE
Greens Haven car park beside Magdalene Fields, Berwick-upon-Tweed

Public toilets
Greens Haven car park

Cafés/pubs
Berwick-upon-Tweed

Terrain
Asphalt paths, pavement and some cobbles

Hilliness
Gently undulating overall; but there is a steep drop to the river after 4 and a steady climb between 6 and 7

Dogs
Dogs welcome but be careful near steep rampart drops. No stiles

Footwear
Year round

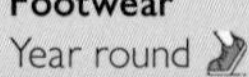

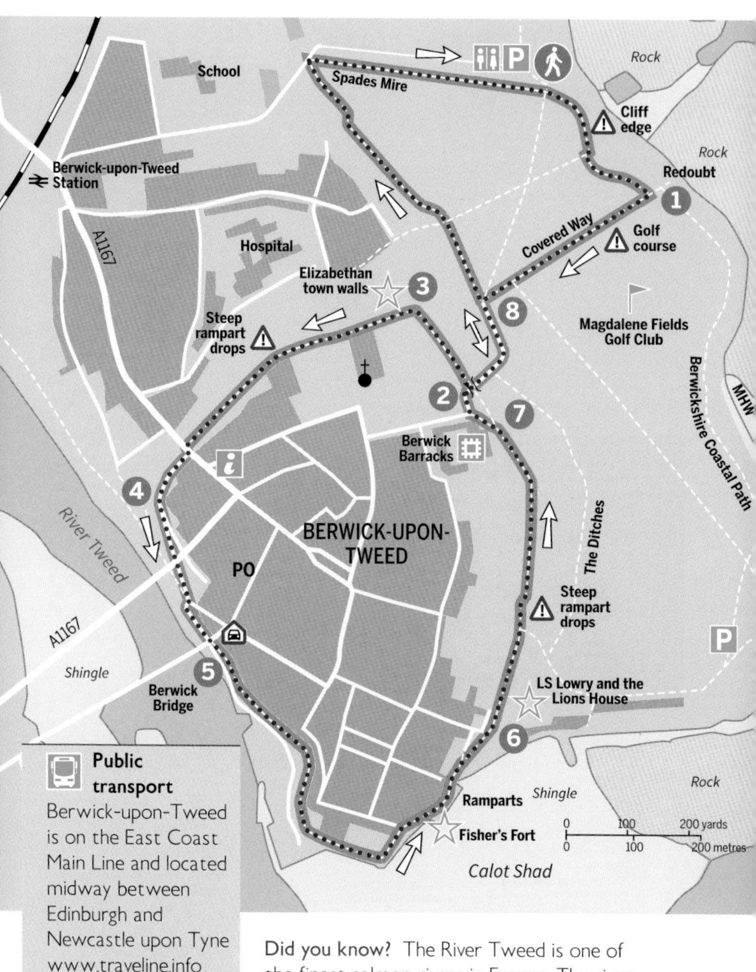

Public transport

Berwick-upon-Tweed is on the East Coast Main Line and located midway between Edinburgh and Newcastle upon Tyne www.traveline.info

Accessibility

Mostly excellent path surfaces, but some inclines might be difficult for self-propelled wheelchairs and there are cobbles between 4 and 5

Did you know? The River Tweed is one of the finest salmon rivers in Europe. The river rises at Tweed's Well in the Lowther Hills and flows for 97 miles across Borders countryside passing though the Scottish towns of Peebles, Galashiels, Melrose and Kelso, before entering Northumberland for the last few miles of its course to reach the North Sea at Berwick. The name Tweed is derived from an Old Celtic term meaning 'border'. The world-famous cloth is named after its long association with the river.

STORIES BEHIND THE WALK

☆ **Elizabethan town walls** Over the centuries, Berwick-upon-Tweed passed from English control to Scottish and back again several times, being retaken by England for the final time in 1482. In 1558, a huge amount of money was spent constructing walls to protect it from further attack by the Scots. An Italian military engineer was brought in and the resulting structure, complete with bastions, is the only one of its kind in Britain.

Berwick Barracks Among the first purpose-built barracks in England, work on the structure started in 1717 in response to the Jacobite rising of 1715. Fearing further uprisings by supporters of the deposed Stuarts, the British government created accommodation here for a full infantry regiment of 600 soldiers plus 36 officers. The Army used the site until 1963. Today, the buildings are open to the public, housing the regimental museum of the King's Own Scottish Borderers as well as other exhibitions.

Cliff edge

Golf course

Elizabethan town walls ☆

½ mile

➡ From car park, look towards sea.
➡ Ignore lane heading right into golf course; instead, take surfaced path along clifftop for 250 yards to path junction.

1 ➡ Turn **right** at crossing of paths. At junction near town walls, turn **left**.
➡ Follow lane round sharp right bend and pass through tunnel (Cowport) in town walls.

2 ➡ Immediately beyond tunnel, go through gate on **right** to access ramparts.
➡ Rise up short incline to path junction at top.

☆ LS Lowry and the Lions House

The artist LS Lowry painted many scenes around Berwick during holidays in the area from the 1930s until the mid-1970s. At one point, he came close to buying the Lions House, a splendid Georgian house overlooking the town walls. Information panels around Berwick show some of Lowry's depictions of the area, enabling those following the 'Lowry Trail' to compare his paintings and sketches with what exists today.

☆ Fisher's Fort

This six-gun battery on the town walls dates from the late 18th century and was designed to protect the mouth of the River Tweed from attack by enemy ships. The cannon seen here today is Russian, captured after the Siege of Sevastopol in 1855 during the Crimean War.

:eep rampart drops between 2 and 4

Berwick Bridge and River Tweed

1 mile

3 ➨ Turn **left**. At next path crossing, turn **left** again.
➨ Keep straight **ahead** until, soon after steps on right, path drops through gate. Follow lane downhill to left bend, beyond which it splits.

4 ➨ Bear **right**. At bottom, bear **right** and follow cobbled lane round to **left**, passing directly above river.
➨ Keep **forward** to road junction (bridge on right).

NATURE NOTES

The River Tweed at Berwick is home to Britain's second largest mute swan colony. There are about 200 birds resident here, rising to as many as 800 in winter. While you're admiring the swans, keep your eyes peeled for herring gulls and for salmon, which are still caught by the traditional 'net and coble' method. Further out to sea, you might be lucky enough to spot bottlenose dolphins. Away from the water, honey bees flit from one town garden to another and can often be seen near the allotments beside the Lions House.

Honey bee

Herring gull

Berwick Barracks

7

LS Lowry and the Lions House

Steep rampart drops

Fisher's Fort

6

1½ miles

5 At road, you'll see two routes on far side. Ignore cobbled lane; keep **left** along higher, paved pedestrian route.
Follow path along top of walls all the way to Fisher's Fort.

6 Soon after cannon at Fisher's Fort, go through gate.
Keep **left** at first fork and then ignore first path dropping left. Keep **ahead** to Berwick Barracks.

Mute swan

Bottlenose dolphin

Salmon

7 ➡ Turn **left** at crossing of paths at far end of barracks. Go through gate and turn **right** along lane.

➡ Follow lane round to **right**, back through Cowport. Round left-hand bend, walk to next junction.

8 ➡ When surfaced routes ahead split, bear **left**. Keep **right** at next fork and continue to lane.

➡ On reaching lane, turn **right**. This leads back to car park.

WALK 2 

BAMBURGH CASTLE

The small village of Bamburgh is dominated by its massive castle, sitting atop a rocky crag. This walk completes a circuit of the imposing complex of buildings, first taking to a sandy trail that looks out beyond wildlife-rich dunes to the Farne Islands. Coming back round the landward side of the fortress, the route crosses the castle green and then heads up into the village – to the grave of the 19th-century heroine Grace Darling and a museum dedicated to her memory.

Distance
1.5 miles/2.4km

Time
1 hour

Start/Finish
Bamburgh

Parking NE69 7BJ
Links Road long-stay car park, Bamburgh

Public toilets
Bamburgh 7

Cafés/pubs
In Bamburgh

Terrain
Pavement through village; sandy trail; surfaced paths

Hilliness
All inclines are relatively gentle

Dogs
Dogs welcome but keep on leads. No stiles

Footwear
Year round

Public transport

The Arriva X18 Newcastle upon Tyne to Berwick-upon-Tweed service stops in Bamburgh. The more local Travelsure 418 service stops in Bamburgh on the circular route between Alnwick, Seahouses and Belford

Accessibility

Surfaced paths and pavements from 5 onwards, but barriers at 6 are an obstruction for wheelchairs/mobility scooters

Did you know? Bamburgh Dunes covers an area of almost 100 acres and is both a Site of Special Scientific Interest – designated in 1995 – and part of the North Northumberland Dunes Special Area of Conservation, a valuable habitat for rare coastal plants and insects and a rich diversity of more common flora and fauna.

Local legend Ghosts said to regularly haunt Bamburgh Castle include: The Pink Lady, believed to be a princess who lived at the castle and was prevented from marrying her true love by her disapproving father; Green Jane, a girl from the village who, it is claimed, slipped, fell and died at the castle while begging for food for her family; and 18th-century Dr John Sharp, who helped restore and care for the castle.

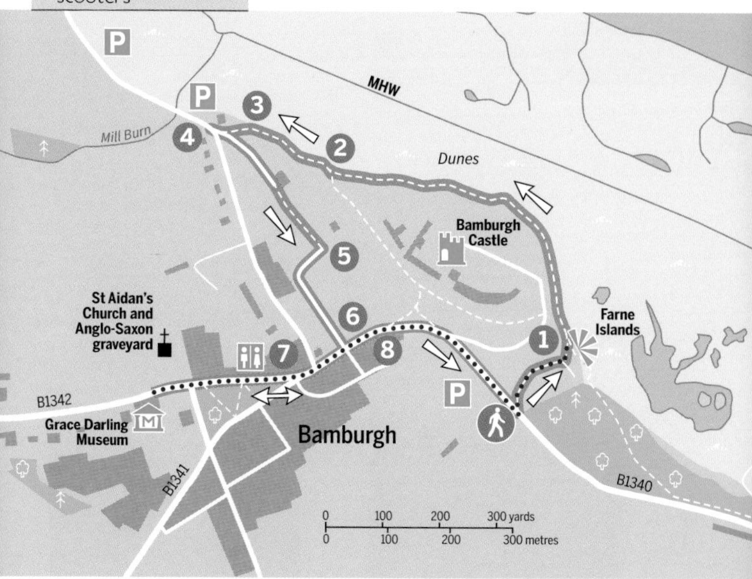

STORIES BEHIND THE WALK

Bamburgh Castle There has been a castle on this site for almost 1,500 years, although the oldest parts of the building that exists today are Norman. In 1894, the Tyneside engineer and industrialist William Armstrong bought the property and went about its restoration. Although his descendants continue to live in the castle today, significant areas of it are open to the public.

Farne Islands This group of tiny islands lies just off the Bamburgh coast. As well as being one of England's most significant grey seal pupping sites, it is an important seabird colony, best known for its puffins. Apart from seasonal National Trust rangers, no one lives on the islands, although past residents have included St Aidan, St Cuthbert and Grace Darling.

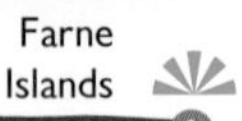

¼ mile

P

➡ Leave car park via vehicle entrance and take track opposite, heading **uphill**.
➡ Reaching car park, cross to grass on far side of asphalt.

1 ➡ Drop **half-left** onto sandy trail beside wooden fence above dunes.
➡ You later lose guiding fence, but trail keeps **straight on**.
➡ Ignore side turnings and continue to clearer path joining from the left, just beyond the far end of castle mound.

Anglo-Saxon graveyard

Archaeologists unearthed dozens of skeletons while working on an Anglo-Saxon graveyard in the dunes near Bamburgh Castle between 1998 and 2007. Examination of the bones suggests many of the bodies are those of high-status individuals who were living in the castle as early as the 7th century. The bodies have since been reinterred in the crypt at St Aidan's Church.

Grace Darling

The daughter of a lighthouse keeper based on the Farne Islands, Grace Darling achieved fame when she helped save nine people from a steamship that had run aground in a storm. A museum in Bamburgh, just yards from the house where she was born, tells the story of the rescue and of Grace's life. She is buried in St Aidan's churchyard opposite.

2 — ½ mile — 3 — 4 — 5 — ¾ mile

2 Keep **ahead** on clearer path.
Continue to waymarker post at next obvious path split.

3 Here, bear **left**, as indicated by waymark.
Walk on to reach a crossing track.

4 Turn **left** along rough track. Route narrows beyond cottages.
Walk round side of barrier to pass beside two sheds.

NATURE NOTES

The first part of the walk passes above the Bamburgh dunes, dominated by marram grass which helps stabilise the sand. Other plant species found here include pyramidal orchids, the pink flowers of which can be seen in June and July. Watch for sparrow-like reed buntings perched on top of bushes and for fork-tailed sand martins darting about. Oystercatchers – large, black-and-white waders – are easily identified by their long, reddish bills and legs.

Reed bunting

Sand martin

St Aidan's Church
Grace Darlin
Museum
Anglo-Saxon graveyard
6
7
1 mile

5 ➡ After passing these, turn **right** along surfaced path round edge of Bamburgh Castle Green.

6 ➡ Pass between barriers on far side of green and turn **right** along pavement.

Oystercatchers

Pyramidal orchid

Marram grass

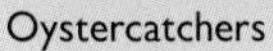

1¼ miles

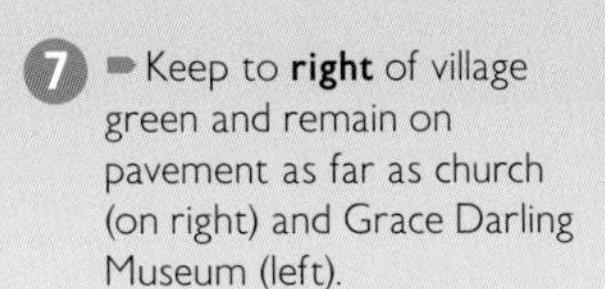

7 Keep to **right** of village green and remain on pavement as far as church (on right) and Grace Darling Museum (left).
After visiting both, retrace steps to 6.

8 Continue on pavement for 50 yards and then cross to other side of main road (B1340).
Continue in same direction. Car park entrance is on **right** in 250 yards.

This page (clockwise): Fisherman's Haven, Berwick-upon-Tweed; gannets at Bamburgh Castle; Craster Harbour; 13th-century gatehouse, Warkworth Castle
Opposite (clockwise): Kielder Water's north shore; Lion Bridge, Alnwick; weathered sand-stone on the moorland edge, Shaftoe Crags

WALK 3

WOOLER COMMON

On the north-eastern edge of the Northumberland National Park, the high tops of the Cheviots give way to an area of lower hills steeped in history. Wander the trails of Wooler Common for a taste of this wonderfully secluded corner of the county. This walk starts from a picnic area beside wildlife-rich ponds, passes through woodland, brushes up against ancient settlements and crosses open commons with good views of distant hills and the coast.

Distance
2.4 miles/3.9km

Time
1½ hours

Start/Finish
Wooler Common, 1 mile south-west of Wooler

Parking NE71 6RL
Forestry England's Wooler Common car park

Public toilets
In nearby Wooler

Cafés/pubs
In nearby Wooler

Terrain
Road; rough tracks; grassy paths; woodland trails; surfaced path

Hilliness
Undulating, with steady ascent from start to 1 and steep descents after 1 and 6

Footwear
Winter
Spring/Autumn
Summer

Dogs
Dogs welcome but on leads on Wooler Common. No stiles

Public transport
None

Accessibility

Short sections on road; surfaced paths beside ponds on Wooler Common; otherwise unsurfaced paths; steps leading onto bridge soon after 1

Did you know? Although associated with wool production since early medieval times, and an important centre for the Northumberland wool trade, the small market town of Wooler's unusual name (Welloure in the 12th century) is believed to come from the Anglo-Saxon 'wella' – a well, spring or stream. Located on the banks of the Wooler Water, the name might mean a 'bank or hill overlooking a stream'.

Local legend In the late 18th and into the 19th century Wooler, in its position at the foot of the Cheviot Hills, became recognised as a health resort for it clean, fresh air. In her youth, Grace Darling (see Walk 2, page 23) stayed in Wooler in an attempt to cure her consumption, while Sir Walter Scott stayed at a local farm, also for health reasons, in 1791.

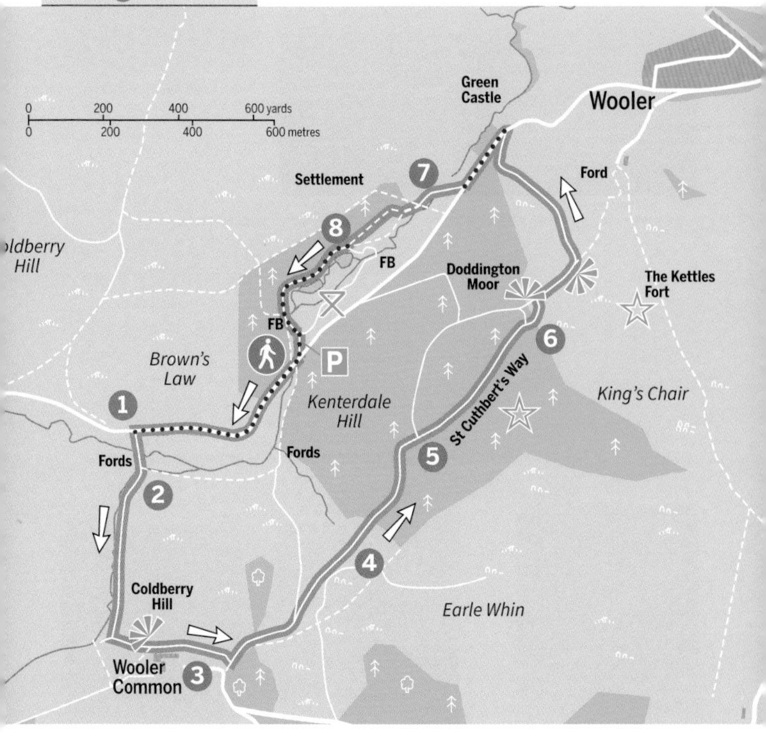

STORIES BEHIND THE WALK

☆ **Prehistoric art** After the route leaves the forest, you're able to look out over the gently rolling hills of eastern Northumberland. The nearest of these is Doddington Moor, covered with even older artefacts than those found on Wooler's hills, including examples of 'rock art' that are possibly 4,000 years old.

☆ **St Cuthbert's Way** Parts of this route follow the St Cuthbert's Way. This popular 62-mile walking route links the two monasteries most closely associated with the 7th-century bishop – Melrose in the Scottish Borders and Lindisfarne, or Holy Island, on the Northumberland coast. The cult of St Cuthbert, strong throughout medieval times, turned these places and his shrine at Durham Cathedral into pilgrimage sites.

½ mile

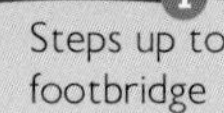

Steps up to footbridge

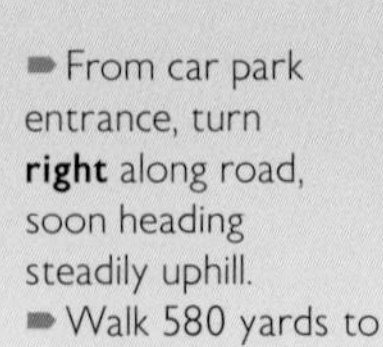

➡ From car park entrance, turn **right** along road, soon heading steadily uphill.
➡ Walk 580 yards to fingerpost on left.

1 ➡ Turn **left** down rough track, descending steeply. Cross footbridge.
➡ After gate, step across tiny burn.

2 ➡ Swing slightly **right** along faint, grassy path beside burn. Ignore track heading on to hill on left.
➡ About 450 yards beyond gate, swing **left** at waymarker post, heading towards cottage.

☆ **Ancient settlements** The hills to the west of Wooler are dotted with the earthwork remains of ancient settlements. Coldberry Hill, seen from the early part of this walk, has two homesteads on its eastern slopes and a field system, all dating from Roman times. As you near 6, you'll also see the ramparts belonging to The Kettles, an Iron Age hillfort.

Coldberry Hill

☆ Reivers

Like many areas on the Anglo-Scottish border, this part of Northumberland suffered greatly at the hands of the Border Reivers between the 13th and 17th centuries. These ruthless clans, who owed allegiance to neither England nor Scotland, went about looting, pillaging, stealing livestock and murdering their enemies.

3 4

1 mile

3 ➨ About 60 yards beyond cottage, bear **left** along narrower but better-defined path.
➨ Walk downhill with fence on right and fork **right** at next waymarker.
➨ Continue to gate.

4 ➨ Enter forest via gate and swing **right**.
➨ Keep **forward** as another path joins from left as you cross open area on Kenterdale Hill.

NATURE NOTES

A wide variety of trees can be seen on this walk, particularly towards the end. These include larch and even Corsican pine on the wooded slopes leading up from the ponds. On the damp ground at the water's edge, you'll see alder, which is able to grow in conditions that would be too wet for most other trees. In early spring, primroses are among the first flowers to bring colour back to Wooler Common. Later, as the weather warms up, adders, the UK's only venomous snake, might be spotted in the long grass.

Corsican pine

Alder

St Cuthbert's Way

Doddington Moor

The Kettles

1½ miles

5 ➨ Nearing more densely forested area again, bear **right** at fork in path.
➨ Follow woodland trail to gate.

6 ➨ Leave forest via gate. Follow winding path **downhill** for 180 yards and then bear **left** at fork.
➨ Walk down to road (with cattle grid, right) and go **left**. In 200 yards, take track on **right**.

Adder

Larch trees grow to 80 feet. Although they produce short needles, they are deciduous. Little pink flowers appear among the needles and these produce red or yellow cones, which go brown when they mature

The primrose is sacred to Freya, Norse god of love, and the five petals on each flower symbolise the stages of life – birth, initiation, consumption, repose and death

Cattle grid

2 miles

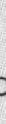

7 ➡ After crossing burn, track swings right. Leave it here by taking grassy path beside fence.

➡ When fence ends, keep to trail along woodland edge.

8 ➡ Keep straight **ahead** when you step up onto surfaced path beside ponds.

➡ Later cross bridge to re-enter car park.

WALK 4

DUNSTANBURGH CASTLE FROM CRASTER

Dunstanburgh Castle is one of the most dramatically situated fortifications in Britain, standing proud on a rocky headland that is battered by the North Sea. This walk approaches it from the pretty little fishing village of Craster, following the coast path for about 1½ miles, in the company of fascinating geological features and a variety of seabirds. After skirting the edge of a golf course, it heads inland to follow a tranquil, meandering route back to the village.

Distance
4.5 miles / 7.3 km

Time
2¼ hours

Start/Finish
Craster

Parking NE66 3TW
Quarry car park, Craster

Public toilets
Quarry car park

Cafés/pubs
Craster

Terrain
Pavement through village; mostly grassy paths; surfaced tracks

Hilliness
Gently undulating with moderate climb up to castle soon after 2

Dogs
Dogs welcome on leads. No stiles

Footwear
Winter
Spring/Autumn
Summer

Did you know? The eider is a northern sea duck, commonly called St Cuthbert's or Cuddy's duck in Northumberland. 'Eider down' is the soft, downy breast feathers of the duck, used by the female to line its nest, and collected by bedware manufacturers for centuries for stuffing quilts – hence eiderdown – and filling pillows.

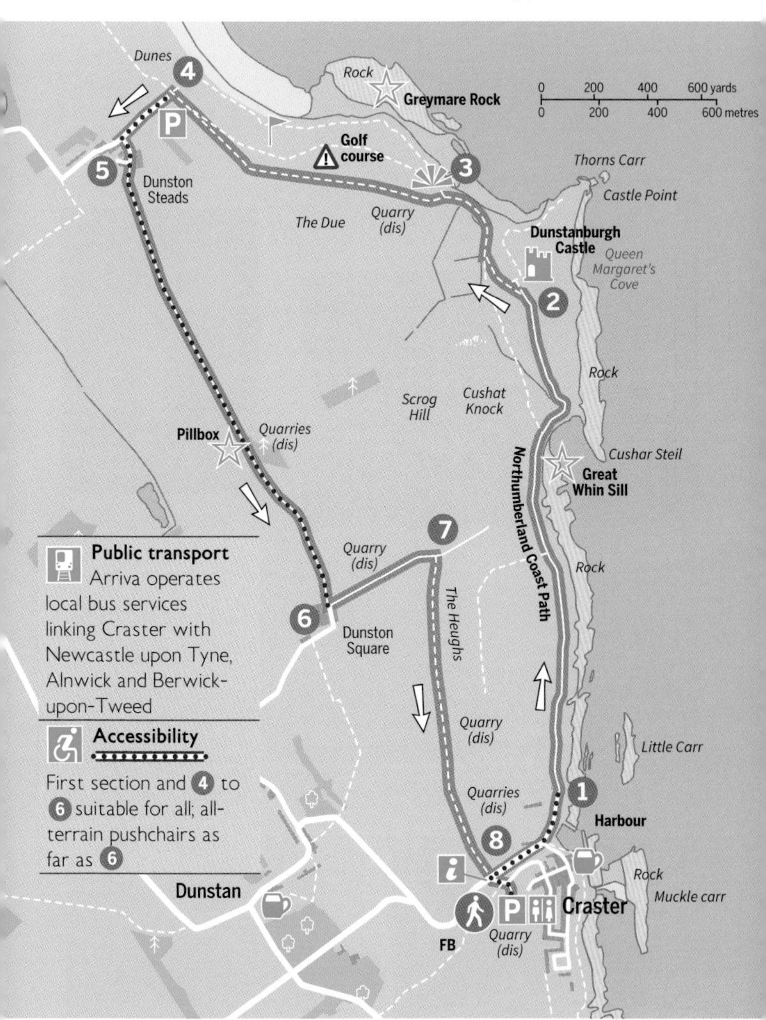

Public transport Arriva operates local bus services linking Craster with Newcastle upon Tyne, Alnwick and Berwick-upon-Tweed

Accessibility

First section and 4 to 6 suitable for all; all-terrain pushchairs as far as 6

STORIES BEHIND THE WALK

Dunstanburgh Castle Earl Thomas of Lancaster had this impressive fortification built in 1313, largely as a symbol of his opposition to King Edward II. After the baron's failed rebellion and execution, the imposing twin-towered gatehouse was strengthened and converted to a keep which featured in an 1828 painting by JMW Turner. The only time it saw military action was in the second half of the 15th century, when it was captured twice by Yorkist forces during the Wars of the Roses.

☆ **Kippers** Craster has long been associated with the production of kippers. Today, the tradition is continued by L Robson & Sons, a family business that uses its 130-year-old smokehouses to turn North Sea herrings, known as 'silver darlings', into kippers. The smoked fish are sold through the family's busy village shop.

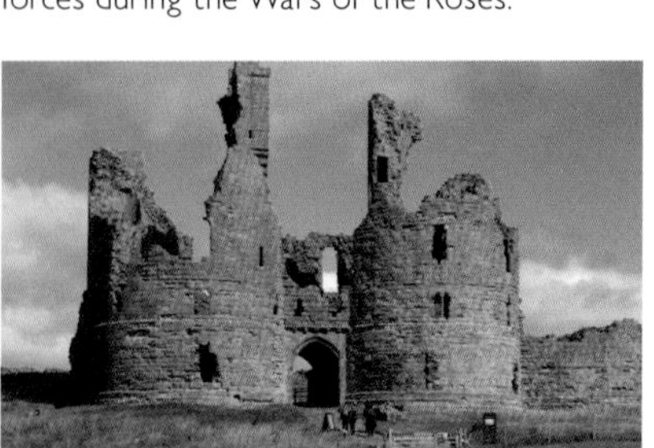

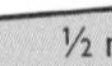

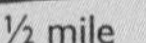

½ mile

Great Whin Sill ☆

1 mile

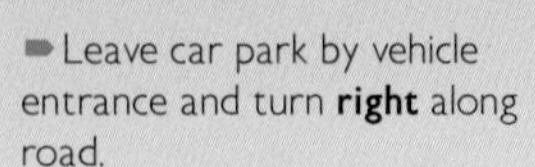

➡ Leave car park by vehicle entrance and turn **right** along road.
➡ With harbour directly ahead, turn **left** along Dunstanburgh Road.
➡ Go through gate at lane-end.

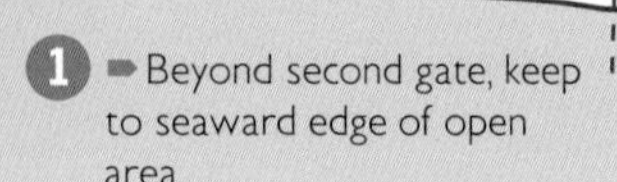

1 ➡ Beyond second gate, keep to seaward edge of open area.
➡ Follow track through two more gates.
➡ 150 yards later, the track swings **left** and becomes grassy path making directly for castle.

☆ **Pillbox** The unusual building beside the track near Scrog Hill is a pillbox, one of several in the Craster area. Dozens of these small fortifications were built all along the Northumberland coast in the early years of World War II when there was a threat of a seaborne invasion by the Nazis. This one was built from concrete-filled sandbags and was fitted with loopholes through which weapons could be fired.

Great Whin Sill

Like Bamburgh Castle further up the coast, and Hadrian's Wall, Dunstanburgh was built on the Great Whin Sill. This dolerite rock was formed millions of years ago when volcanic activity resulted in magma being forced between beds of existing rock. As the magma then cooled, it crystallised and shrank, forming hexagonal columns.

Dunstanburgh Castle
Greymare Rock
Golf course
1½ miles
2 miles

2 ➡ Immediately before gate into castle compound, take trail on **left**.
➡ Soon this joins track from left. Go through gate onto golf course.

3 ➡ Continue for 50 yards and then veer **left** around edge of green, aiming for wooden post.
➡ Join clear path. Bear **left** at two forks, staying near fence along edge of golf course for almost ¾ mile to reach a gate on left.

NATURE NOTES

You'll inevitably spot lots of birds as you walk the coast path from Craster. Among these are the kittiwake, a species of medium-sized, cliff-nesting gull; the razorbill, a black-and-white seabird related to the puffin; and the eider, sometimes known locally as Cuddy ducks. Gorse, with its spiky leaves and brilliant yellow flowers, is a common feature throughout the walk. The distinctive rock formation just beyond the castle, Greymare Rock, consists of layers of limestone warped by heat and pressure caused by the same volcanic activity that created the Great Whin Sill.

Kittiwake

Above: Gorse
Left: Greymare Rock

4 ➨ Turn **left** through gate.
➨ Follow lane **uphill**. On reaching first buildings, take lane on **left**.

5 ➨ On far side of cottages, as surfaced track bends right, bear **left** to take track to right of farm building. This soon becomes a concrete road.
➨ Follow it for more than 1 mile to a cluster of farm buildings.

Eider ducks (male, left; female, right) can be seen around the northern and eastern coasts of Britain. They are sea ducks, eating mussels and other shellfish

The razorbill is an expert diver and has short, stubby wings, as much adapted for swimming as flying. The razorbill spends much of its life at sea, coming to land only to breed

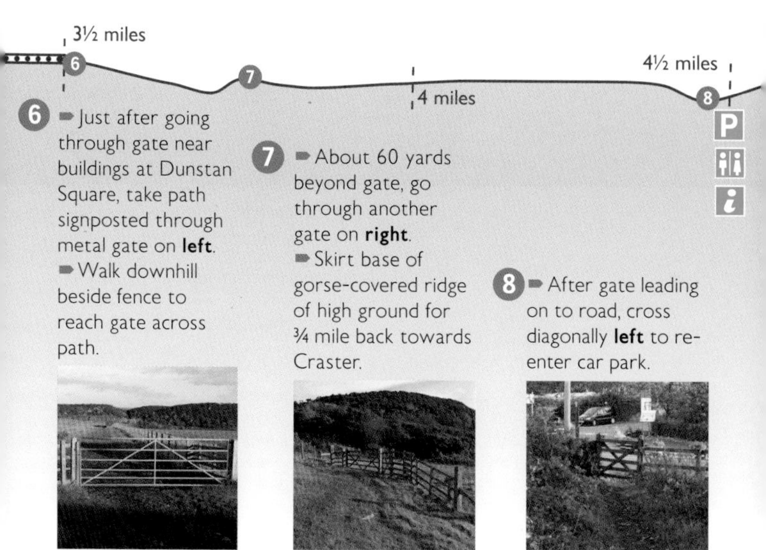

6 ➡ Just after going through gate near buildings at Dunstan Square, take path signposted through metal gate on **left**.
➡ Walk downhill beside fence to reach gate across path.

7 ➡ About 60 yards beyond gate, go through another gate on **right**.
➡ Skirt base of gorse-covered ridge of high ground for ¾ mile back towards Craster.

8 ➡ After gate leading on to road, cross diagonally **left** to re-enter car park.

Opposite (clockwise): eider duck; beech tree mast; pyramdial orchid
This page (clockwise): fieldfare; poppy; osprey; oak tree

WALK 5

ALNWICK

Like many Northumberland settlements, Alnwick is dominated by its castle, Great Britain's second-largest inhabited castle after Windsor. Views of this substantial fortification come and go from the riverside section of this lovely walk. This is also where walkers are most likely to see wildlife as the paths brush up against the River Aln, cross fields and meander through patches of woodland. The route also passes close to the award-winning Alnwick Garden.

Distance
3.5 miles/5.6km

Time
1¾ hours

Start/Finish
Alnwick

Parking NE66 1SF
Greenwell Road car park, Alnwick

Public toilets
Greenwell Road

Cafés/pubs
Alnwick

Terrain
Pavement through town; surfaced paths; unsurfaced field paths beside river

Hilliness
Steady descent from 2 to 4; short incline at 6; longer climb from Lion Bridge

Dogs
Dogs welcome on leads. No stiles

Footwear
Winter
Spring/Autumn
Summer

Public transport Alnmouth Station (East Coast Main Line) is about 3 miles east of Alnwick and a regular bus service runs between the two. National Express and Arriva bus services also connect Alnwick with Newcastle upon Tyne and Berwick-upon-Tweed

Accessibility Early sections through town and path to 4 suitable for all, then from Lion Bridge

Did you know? In the films of *Harry Potter and the Philosopher's Stone* (2001) and *Harry Potter and the Chamber of Secrets* (2002), Alnwick Castle had a starring role as Hogwarts School of Witchcraft and Wizardry. The Outer Bailey was the setting for Madam Hooch's broomstick-flying lessons and Harry and his classmates played Quidditch there (with the help of a model of the castle and some super-clever filming techniques). The castle's Lion Arch was used to film scenes of Harry and friends on their way to and from visits to Hagrid's Cabin and the Forbidden Forest, while other doorways and courtyards were backgrounds for students and staff going about their daily business, and Harry and Ron crash-landed the Weasley family's flying car in the Inner Bailey.

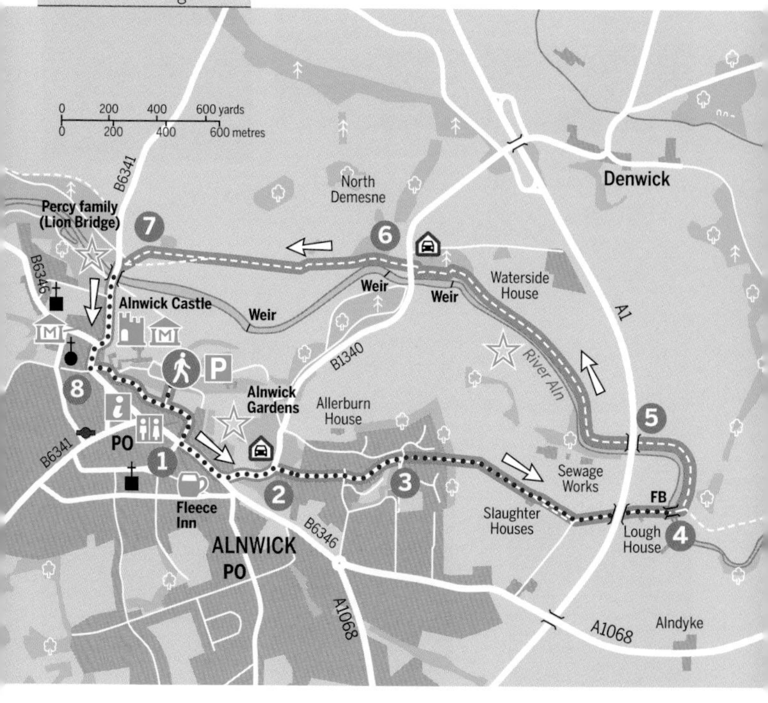

STORIES BEHIND THE WALK

☆ **River Aln** The River Aln rises on the eastern edge of the Cheviot Hills and enters the sea at Alnmouth, just downstream of Alnwick. With the help of money from the EU, work has been carried out along the river to improve fish and eel migration. This has included the installation of passes to enable the fish and eels to swim round weirs and other obstructions that stand in the way of them reaching their spawning grounds in the river's upper reaches.

☆ Percy family

Alnwick has been the seat of the Percy family, descended from Norman noblemen, for more than 700 years. One of the best-known members was Sir Henry Percy, born in the 1360s and one of the key characters in Shakespeare's *Henry IV (Part I)*. He was nicknamed Hotspur for his speedy advances against the Scots during cross-border conflicts.

Fleece Inn

➡ Leave car park and turn **left** along Greenwell Road, following it to main road.

1 ➡ At T-junction opposite Fleece Inn, turn **left** along Bondgate Without (B6346).
➡ Take next road on **left** (B1340, signposted Bamburgh), walking for 200 yards to fingerpost on Fisher Lane.

2 ➡ Turn **right**, rising along lane.
➡ Keep **straight on** when lane narrows.
➡ Continue for 450 yards to road.

Alnwick Gardens

Construction on the Duchess of Northumberland's Alnwick Garden began in 2000. Now a popular tourist attraction, it contains the world's largest Japanese cherry orchard as well as impressive water features, the massive Treehouse Restaurant and the Poison Garden, which is accessible only on a guided tour.

Alnwick Castle

Alnwick Castle is the home of the Duke and Duchess of Northumberland, Ralph and Jane Percy. The building dates from the 14th century, although it fell into disrepair in the 17th century. Subsequent periods of restoration introduced Gothic elements, a mock-medieval exterior and Italianate features. The castle is open to the public.

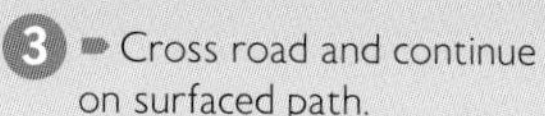

3 ➠ Cross road and continue on surfaced path.
➠ This later bends **left** and then **right**, becoming broader. Pass under A1 and walk round side of locked gate to reach footbridge.

4 ➠ Cross Peter's Mill footbridge over River Aln.
➠ Turn **left** along riverside trail, soon entering field via gate, and keep on to meet A1 again.

NATURE NOTES

Keep your eyes peeled for wildlife as you walk beside the River Aln. Herons stand at the water's edge, while dippers bob up and down on rocks mid-stream. The field after 5 is covered with molehills, but you're unlikely to spot the creatures that created these piles of earth because they spend much of their lives underground. There are several old oaks near 7. Watch for nuthatches scurrying up and down their trunks in search of food.

Above: heron
Left: dipper

5 ➡ Path passes back under A1. Continue along riverbank, later entering woodland.
➡ Carefully cross B1340 road and go through kissing-gate opposite.
➡ Keep **forward** to path Y-junction.

6 ➡ Bear **left** when trail splits.
➡ Nearing fence, swing **right** and go through kissing-gate. Faint trail runs parallel with fence on right: follow it for nearly ½ mile to a path fork.

Characteristically, nuthatches move headfirst down a tree trunk. They live in mature deciduous woodland, mainly eating hazel nuts, beech mast and acorns which they wedge into bark crevices and split with blows from their sharp beak

Oak tree

Mole hills

Percy family (Lion Bridge)

Alnwick Castle

3 miles

3½ miles

7 ➨ Here, bear **left** to drop towards Lion Bridge.
➨ Turn **left** at road. At top of rise, keep close to castle walls and walk down Narrowgate.

8 ➨ Just before road swings left, go **left** into Bow Alley.
➨ When cobbles end, head up asphalted slope on **right**. This leads back into Greenwell Road.

WALK 6 CATCH A BUS

WARKWORTH

In a county with lots of lovely villages, medieval Warkworth stands out as one of the prettiest. This walk starts from the edge of coastal dunes and then follows a riverside path, fringed by woodland. After a short climb, sea views come and go as walkers make their way to the castle ruins that dominate this little loop on the River Coquet. The route ends with a gentle stroll down through the village, home to several pubs and cafés.

Distance 2.9 miles/4.7km
Time 1½ hours
Start/Finish Warkworth
Parking NE65 0SW Warkworth Beach car park, signed from the main road bridge at the north end of the village, 650 yards east of the A1068
Public toilets Warkworth Beach car park; Warkworth Castle
Cafés/pubs Warkworth
Terrain Mostly surfaced paths; pavement through village
Hilliness Moderately steep descent to river near start and between 7 and 8; steep ascent after 4
Dogs Dogs welcome but keep on leads. No stiles
Footwear Year round

Public transport Arriva operates two regular bus services stopping at Warkworth: Berwick-upon-Tweed to Newcastle upon Tyne and Alnwick to Newcastle upon Tyne: www.arrivabus.co.uk

Accessibility

Suitable for all-terrain pushchairs except for steps soon after 6; village pavements and section between 2 and 3 suitable for wheelchairs and mobility scooters

Did you know? Built in local stone in the late 14th century, Warkworth Bridge is a Grade II Listed structure. Its solid-looking, defensive arched gateway marks it out as the only surviving fortified bridge in England. A sharply angled central cutwater forms the two-arched span, each arch being 59 feet across.

Local legend Known as the Grey Lady, the ghost of Margaret Neville, who was born at Warkworth in the late 13th century, has been seen wandering the castle ruins. The ghost of a young man is also said to have been seen along the castle walls.

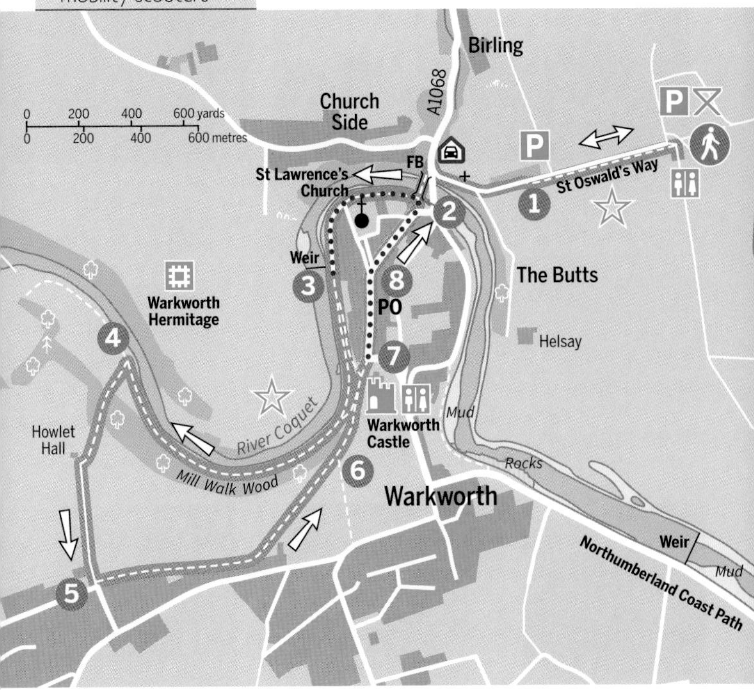

STORIES BEHIND THE WALK

St Lawrence's Church There was a church on the site of St Lawrence's as early as the 8th century, but this timber structure was probably destroyed by the Vikings. The construction of the stone church began in about 1132, the building doubling up as a place of refuge for villagers whenever Scottish raiders descended on the area.

☆ St Oswald's Way
Parts of this walk follow the St Oswald's Way. This 97-mile walking route from Lindisfarne (Holy Island) to Heavenfield on Hadrian's Wall links sites associated with Oswald, a 7th-century king of Northumbria who helped bring Christianity to the area.

St Oswald's Way
½ mile
St Lawrence's Church

➡ With your back to toilet block, turn **right** along asphalt and immediately take trail through hedges on **left**.
➡ Cross driveway to join path along field edge, walking for 400 yards to road.

1 ➡ When path emerges on road, continue in same direction.
➡ Cross A1068 and turn **left**. Pass over footbridge.

2 ➡ Immediately after stone archway, turn **right** along surfaced, riverside path.
➡ Continue past church, where path opens out to lane, and keep **forward** to lane-end.

Warkworth Castle

The substantial ruins of the medieval Warkworth Castle crown a small hilltop overlooking the village. The castle walls are largely intact as is the impressive cross-shaped keep, which dates from the late 14th century. It's hardly surprising then that this sturdy powerhouse withstood several Scottish attacks. The ruins, now in the care of English Heritage, are open to the public all year round (only weekends in winter).

☆ River Coquet

The River Coquet rises at Chew Green, the Roman camp on the modern border between England and Scotland. It comes rushing down from the Cheviot Hills and then meanders its way through a beautiful dale. When it reaches Warkworth, it is entering the final stages of its journey, eventually emptying into the North Sea at nearby Amble.

Warkworth Hermitage (opposite bank)

River Coquet ☆

4

1 mile

3 ➡ At far end of lane, follow narrowing riverside trail between wooden posts.
➡ Enjoy riverside path for just over ½ mile to fingerposted T-junction.

4 ➡ Drawing level with Warkworth Hermitage on far side of river, turn **left** at T-junction.
➡ At lane junction, go **left** again. Continue to 'give way' sign.

NATURE NOTES

As you set off along the field path at the start of the walk, the hawthorn hedges on the right are covered in white flowers in spring; then, later in the summer, poppies often appear along the field edge. The churchyard contains several carefully tended yews while the woodland along the riverbank has a 'wilder' feel to it, blanketed in its early stages by ivy and later dominated by sycamore trees.

Hawthorn is England's most common hedgerow bush, being a popular choice for hedging when fields were first enclosed more than 300 years ago. Often known as May, after the month in which it flowers, the blossom heralds the arrival of summer – hence the expression 'Never cast a clout, 'til May is out', meaning keep your winter wardrobe at hand until May is in bloom

5

1½ miles

Warkworth Castle

6

2 miles

5 ➡ Behind 'give way' sign, take path through field on **left**.
➡ On entering play area, cross diagonally **left** to leave via kissing-gate.
➡ Follow grassy trod to next path junction.

6 ➡ Go **left** along gravel path, passing between fence and wall.
➡ Quickly bear **right** along top of embankment and, in 90 yards, descend steps near castle.

Often found in churchyards, the yew is an evergreen associated with great longevity and a symbol of faith. Almost every part of the tree is poisonous. In medieval times, its strong and pliable wood was used for making longbows

The sycamore is member of the maple family and fully grown trees can exceed 100 feet

Ivy's closely packed leaves make the perfect hibernation habitat for many over-wintering insects

St Oswald's Way

2½ miles

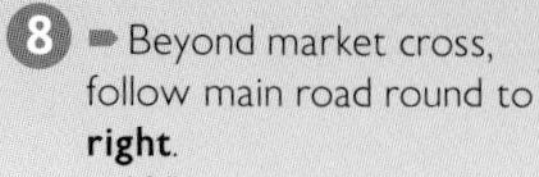

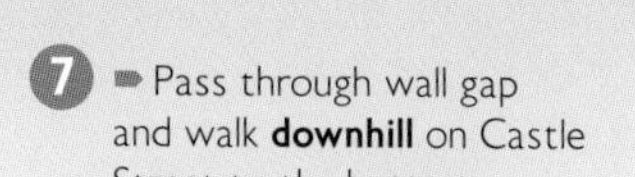

7 ➡ Pass through wall gap and walk **downhill** on Castle Street to the bottom.

8 ➡ Beyond market cross, follow main road round to **right**.
➡ When pavement ends, keep **straight on**, passing through stone archway at **2**.
➡ Retrace steps to car park.

WALK 7

KIELDER WATER

The power of humans to tame nature and create landscapes is evident throughout this walk at Kielder Water and Forest Park. A meandering and well-waymarked stroll near the shores of the huge reservoir is followed by a walk among the towering conifers of the immense plantations. Don't let the artificial origins of the surroundings put you off though – nature has adapted, and you'll see wildlife here as well as scenery on a monumental scale.

Distance
4 miles/6.4km

Time
2 hours

Start/Finish
Kielder Water

Parking NE48 1BH
Hawkhope car park, Falstone

Public toilets
Hawkhope car park

Cafés/pubs
In nearby Falstone

Terrain
Bike path on outward route; forest track on return; rougher path linking them

Hilliness
Gently undulating overall but with sustained gradual ascents between 3 and 4 and between 5 and 6

Dogs
Dogs welcome. No stiles

Footwear
Year round

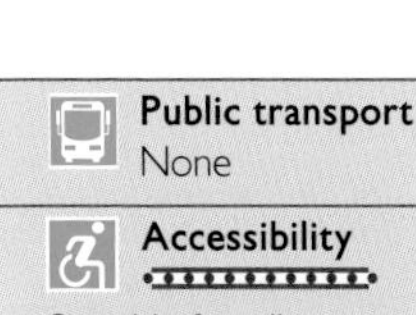

Public transport
None

Accessibility

Suitable for all-terrain pushchairs; mobility scooters and some wheelchairs as far as 3. The section from 4 to the end would be suitable too, but there is a barrier across the track just before 7

Did you know? Kielder Water and Forest are part of the massive 580-square mile Northumberland International Dark Sky Park, the second largest such protected night sky area in Europe. The Campaign to Protect Rural England (CPRE) has rated Kielder as the best place to observe the stars in England. Its remote location far from sources of light pollution means that on a clear night under the right conditions it is so dark that Jupiter and the Milky Way can cast shadows, a phenomenon rarely seen elsewhere in Great Britain.

Local legend It is a complete myth that a 'lost village' lies drowned beneath the waters of Kielder Reservoir. Any buildings that existed in the area of the North Tyne valley that was flooded were dismantled and all materials removed before the water level rose.

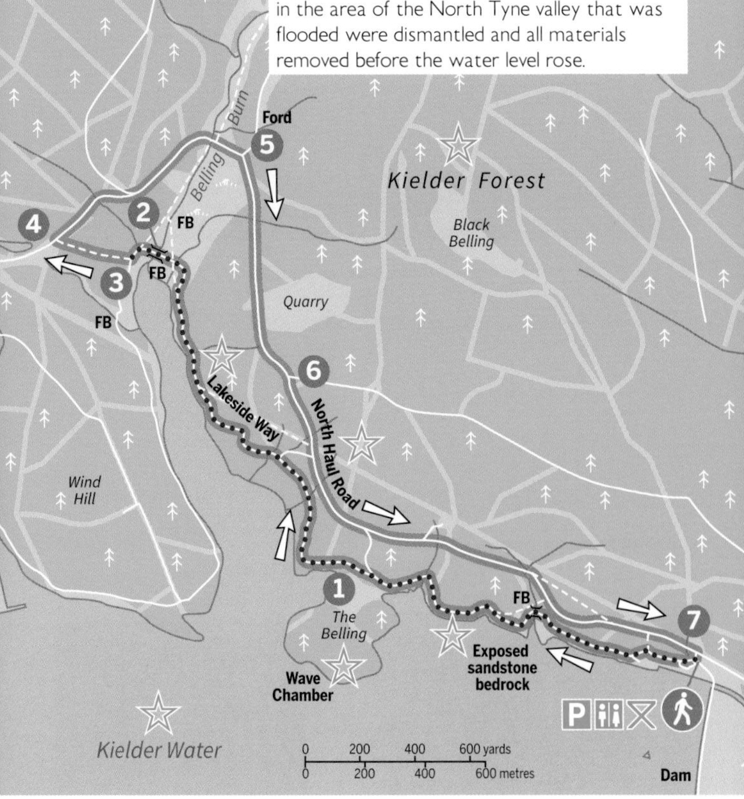

STORIES BEHIND THE WALK

☆ **Kielder Forest** The reservoir is surrounded by sprawling plantations that straddle England's border with Scotland. Like many of the original Forestry Commission sites, it was created during the 1920s. Woodland resources had been severely depleted by World War I, particularly by trench warfare, so there was a need to rebuild and maintain a strategic timber reserve. The Forestry Act came into force in 1919, giving the new commission a lot of freedom to acquire and plant land.

☆ **Lakeside Way**
This waymarked, 26-mile route completes a full circuit of Kielder Water, one of the largest artificial lakes in northern Europe. Surfaced throughout, it is suitable for walkers, cyclists, horse riders, mobility scooters and wheelchair users.

➠ Walk to end of car park furthest from dam and, from right-hand edge, take clear, broad path – waymarked Lakeside Way.
➠ Stay with this clear path for ¾ mile to 'Wave Chamber' sign.

1 ➠ To see the *Wave Chamber*, detour **left** on rougher path (about ½ mile there and back – well worth a visit; see 'Art in the forest', page 57).
➠ Main route keeps **straight on** to footbridge in just over ¾ mile.

☆ Art in the forest

There are dozens of art installations and unusual architectural features scattered throughout Kielder Forest. Created by land artist Chris Drury in 1996, the 'Wave Chamber' is a beehive-like hut built using traditional dry-stone walling techniques. A mirror and lens project an image of the reservoir's waves on to the floor of the tiny building, an impressive sight made more dramatic by the amplified sound on windy days.

☆ Kielder Water

Capable of holding 44 billion gallons, Kielder Water is the Great Britain's largest man-made reservoir by capacity. It was created by damming the headwaters of the River North Tyne near Falstone. Construction began in 1975 and about 100 people had to be moved out of the valley before it was flooded. The Queen opened the site in 1982.

2 ➨ The Lakeside Way crosses bridge over Belling Burn, swings **left** and begins climbing.
➨ Continue another 125 yards beyond bridge to path T-junction.

3 ➨ Turn **right** along path climbing between trees. (There are wooden railings just to right of where path starts.)
➨ Walk to the top of the rise.

NATURE NOTES

Ospreys have been nesting at Kielder Water since 2009. These fish-eating birds of prey can be seen anywhere on the reservoir, but some of their favourite hunting areas are near the dam. You'll see bracken growing beside the Lakeside Way and there is exposed bedrock, including sandstone, at the water's edge. Among the trees planted in this part of Kielder Forest is the Scots pine, the seeds of which are loved by red squirrels. Although extinct in much of England, these native rodents continue to thrive here.

Scots pine

Sandstone

North Haul Road ☆

5 6

2 miles

2½ miles

4 ➨ At top, turn **right** along broad forest road.

➨ This re-crosses Belling Burn and then begins to climb to reach track junction.

5 ➨ Bear **right** at junction where another forest drive joins from left (North Haul Road on map, followed back to car park).

➨ Stride out for almost ½ mile to next forest road junction, ignoring lesser side turning on left as road steadily climbs.

Red squirrel

Above: osprey
Below: bracken

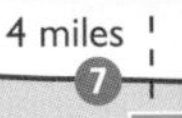

6 ➡ As road then starts descending, keep **right** as another track goes left.
➡ Follow North Haul Road for just over 1 mile to a barrier.

7 ➡ About 80 yards after barrier across track, turn **right** along asphalt lane and immediately **right** again to re-enter car park.

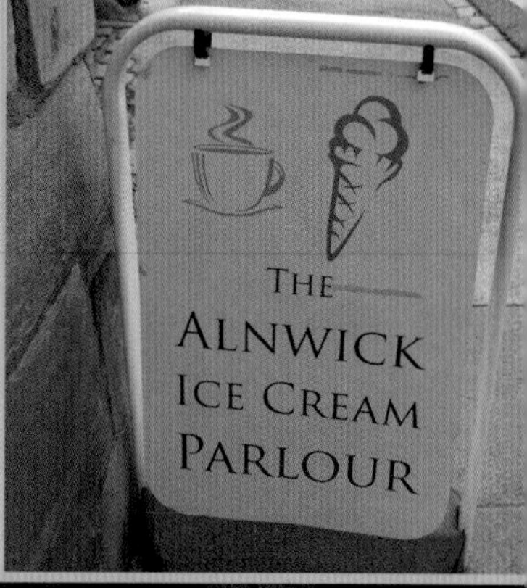

Opposite (clockwise): The Cottage Inn, Dunstan; Castle Brew House, Warkworth. This page (clockwise): The Jolly Fisherman, Craster; Alnwick Ice Cream Parlour; Kippers being smoked; Picnic bench, Cawfields, Hadrian's Wall; The Wynding Inn, Lord Crewe Hotel, Bamburgh

The Cottage Inn
CASTLE BREW HOUSE
Public Bar

WALK 8

SHAFTOE CRAGS

Shaftoe Crags forms part of a line of sandstone hills running through central Northumberland. Weathered rocks, carved by the elements into fantastic shapes, thrust up through the grass and bracken that cover this area of moorland, easily reached from the Bolam Lake car parks. Although the highest point is only 699 feet above sea level, there's nothing else of a similar height nearby, so the paths followed on this walk enjoy far-reaching views.

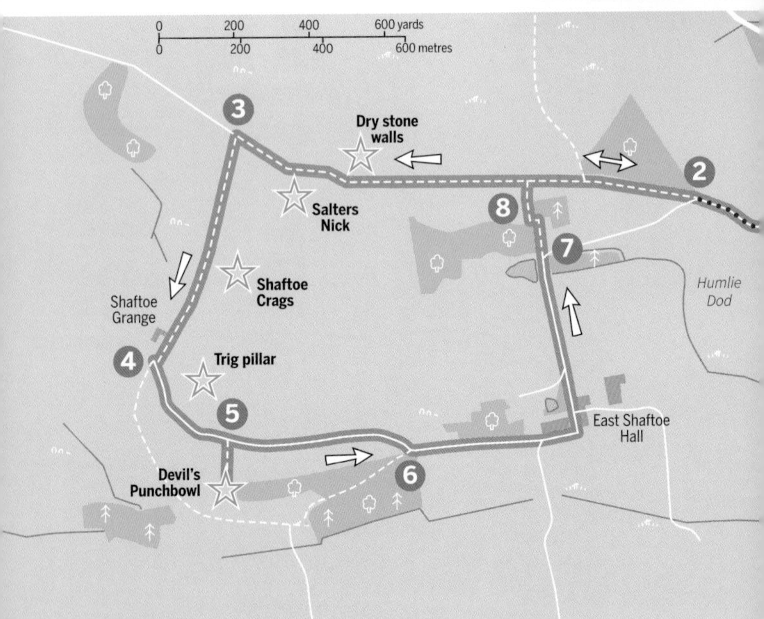

Local legend Legend has it that a fugitive earl, with links to the Jacobite uprising of 1715, hid from pursuing soldiers among the rocky outcrops at Salters Nick to give them the slip.

Distance
4.8 miles/7.7km

Time
2½ hours

Start/Finish
Bolam Lake Country Park, 2½ miles north-west of Belsay

Parking NE20 0HG
West Wood car park, Scot's Gap road – most westerly of the car parks

Public toilets
Bolam Lake's Boathouse Wood car park

Cafés/pubs
Café at visitor centre, Boathouse Wood car park

Terrain
Road; rough tracks; open, grassy moorland; muddy in places

Hilliness
Gently undulating with steeper, rougher descent through Salters Nick before 3

Dogs
Dogs welcome but keep on leads. No stiles

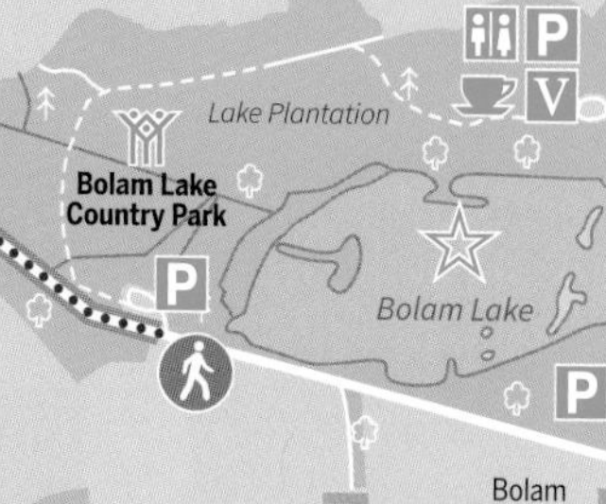

Footwear
Year round

Public transport
None

Accessibility
Road section suitable for wheelchairs; mobility scooters might get as far as 2; all-terrain pushchairs as far as Salters Nick

STORIES BEHIND THE WALK

☆ **Bolam Lake** Local landowner John Beresford commissioned architect John Dobson, best known for his work in Newcastle city centre, to create Bolam Lake and the surrounding woodland for him in 1816. Beresford, later Lord Decies, wanted to provide employment for local people who were struggling during a period of economic decline and paid them one shilling a day to work on the project. The lake and woods are today managed by Northumberland County Council as a country park.

☆ **Geology** The rock outcrops on Shaftoe Crags are composed of sandstone, an arc of which curves down through Northumberland between the coast and the Cheviot Hills. The sedimentary rock forms a series of flat-topped ridges with distinctive craggy outcrops, many of which have been carved into interesting shapes by weathering processes.

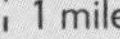

➡ Leave the car park and turn **right** along the road.
➡ Continue for about ½ mile to road junction.

1 ➡ At the crossing of ways, turn **left** along track in front of postbox.
➡ Stay on track for just under ½ mile to cattle grid with gate.

2 ➡ After this, leave track by keeping straight **ahead**, walking on grass beside wall on right.
➡ Later, go through gate and continue with wall all the way to next gate.

☆ Dry stone walls

The low moorland surrounding Shaftoe Crags is enclosed by dry stone walls, an unobtrusive yet common feature of the countryside throughout the north of England. Some date from medieval times, although long, straight walls typical of the higher ground are more closely associated with the enclosure acts of the 18th and 19th centuries. Note how the walls are built without any mortar; stability is achieved through traditional construction methods.

☆ **Trig pillar** At 699 feet above sea level, the trig point, or triangulation pillar, marks the highest point on the moorland. (This is about 90 yards off route.) Ordnance Survey trig pillars like this one started appearing in the British countryside in 1936. They were designed to hold the theodolites used by surveyors creating accurate maps of Great Britain.

Dry stone walls ☆ — Salters Nick ☆ — 3 — Shaftoe Crags ☆ — Shaftoe Grange — 4 ☆

1½ miles — 2 miles

3 ➨ Don't go through next gate; instead, turn **left**, walking with another wall on your right.
➨ Continue until property on right.

4 ➨ Immediately after building (Shaftoe Grange), take rising track on **left**.
➨ Keep **right** when this forks in 175 yards. Or detour left to trig pillar, the hill highpoint.

NATURE NOTES

Above: silver birch
Right: one of Britain's smallest birds, the wren's high-pitched song is one of the loudest and most beautiful

In autumn and winter, you'll see flocks of thrush-sized birds flitting from one tree to another on the road walk from Bolam Lake. These are fieldfares, winter visitors from Scandinavia. Watch too for tiny, fluffed-up wrens along the track leading to the moorland. Some of the beech trees lining this track have patches of lichen on their lower trucks, a sign of good air quality. As you head out onto the open ground, there are silver birch trees on the far side of the wall. The spur path from 5 leads directly to some interesting, weathered sandstone blocks. The largest is the Devil's Punchbowl, with Piper's Chair nearby.

Devil's Punchbowl

2½ miles — 6 — 3 miles — East Shaftoe Hall — 7 — 8 — 3½ miles

5 ➡ About 120 yards beyond fork, take grassy trail on **right** to visit wind-carved rocks.
➡ After exploring them, return to track and turn **right**. Continue to field gate.

6 ➡ Follow track through gate to reach cattle grid.
➡ About 90 yards after cattle grid, follow track round to **left** passing buildings at East Shaftoe Hall.

Top left: sandstone
Top right: lichen
Above: maidenhair spleenwort
Left: fieldfare

7 ➨ Soon after second cattle grid, as track bends right, keep **straight on** – along route climbing beside wall.
➨ At fenced woodland, go **left** and immediately **right**.

8 ➨ From the last fence corner, continue in same direction across open ground (no path) to reach wall part way between 2 and 3.
➨ Turn **right**, this time keep wall on left and retrace steps to car park.

WALK 9 CATCH A BUS (the AD122)

HADRIAN'S WALL

No visit to Northumberland would be complete without a walk beside Hadrian's Wall. This route follows only a short stretch of the iconic Roman structure, but it's a fascinating one. History and landscape come together in a unique way as you follow the wildly undulating ridge on which the wall was built. You pass a milecastle and a turret along the way and enjoy glimpses into the lonely borderlands as well as views of the North Pennines. This is a there-and-back route, fully justified for the awesome views in both directions. Feel free to about turn at any point or, if you are feeling energetic, follow Hadrian's Wall a little further than suggested.

Distance
2.6 miles/4.2km

Time
1¾ hours

Start/Finish
Cawfields, 1¾ miles north of Haltwhistle

Parking NE49 9NN
Cawfields Quarry car park

Public toilets
Cawfields Quarry car park

Cafés/pubs
In nearby Haltwhistle

Terrain
Short section of surfaced path, then undulating, grassy ridge

Hilliness
Ups and downs, some very steep

Footwear
Year round

ROMAN CAMPS

Quar
poo

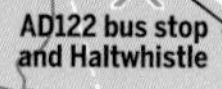

Dogs Dogs welcome but keep on leads. One awkward stile at 5

Public transport None. Rail and bus services available from Haltwhistle, 2½ miles south of start point. The Hadrian's Wall AD122 bus service runs Easter to September only, stopping at the Milestone Inn on B6318, leaving a 600-yard walk north to Cawfields Quarry: hadrianswallcountry.co.uk/travel/bus

Accessibility Excellent on path beside quarry pool to 1; otherwise unsuitable for wheelchairs/pushchairs

Did you know? As part of the Frontiers of the Roman Empire, Hadrian's Wall is a UNESCO World Heritage Site. Past quarrying activity has destroyed part of the wall either side of the Caw Gap, at 6 on this walk, but Milecastle 42, on a steep south-facing slope 2, and the adjacent section of Hadrian's empire frontier to the west and east of it is one of the best-preserved sections of the wall.

Did you know? Cawfields Milecastle (number 42) is said to be haunted by a legionnaire, the apparition apparently patrolling in Roman armour and hovering above the wall, which would have been several feet higher than today's level when first built.

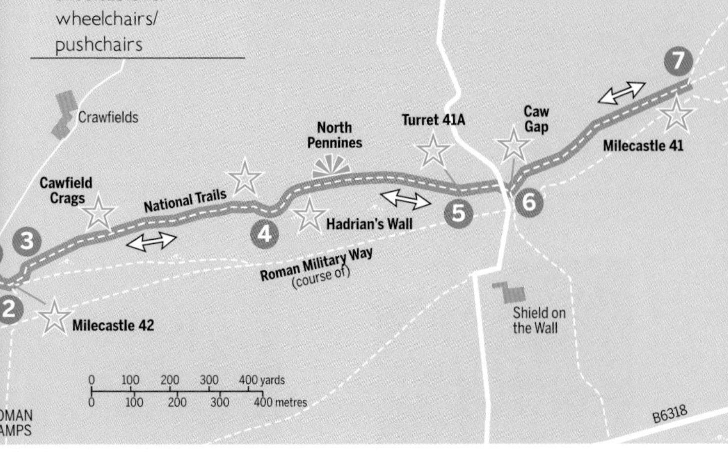

STORIES BEHIND THE WALK

☆ **Hadrian's Wall** It was in AD122, while on a visit to Britain, that the Emperor Hadrian ordered a defensive wall to be built along the edge of the empire's most north-westerly outpost. In particular, he wanted to create a barrier between Roman-controlled Britannia and the Pictish tribes to the north, whose raids had long been a thorn in the side of the occupying forces. The resulting wall stretched for 80 Roman miles (73 modern miles) from the North Sea coast in the east to the Solway Firth in the west.

☆ **National Trails**
Our walk follows the route of two publicly financed long-distance paths, or National Trails. These are the 84-mile Hadrian's Wall Path, from Bowness-on-Solway in Cumbria to Wallsend in Newcastle, and the 268-mile Pennine Way which runs from Edale in Derbyshire to Kirk Yetholm in the Scottish Borders. National Trail routes are marked by white acorn symbols.

Quarry pool ☆ — 1 — 2 ☆ Milecastle 42 — 3 — ¼ mile — ☆ Crawfield Crags — ½ mile — ☆ Hadrian's Wall; National Trails — 4

➡Take path skirting left-hand edge of quarry pool, later reaching a kissing-gate.

1 ➡Go through kissing-gate. ➡Bear **right** to climb grassy slope, soon joining track leading up to next set of gates.

☆ Milecastles and turrets

Small forts, or milecastles, were built at intervals of roughly one Roman mile along the entire length of Hadrian's Wall. Each had a gateway through which people and goods would have passed on their way in and out of the Roman-controlled region. The walls and gateway at Cawfields (milecastle number 42) are still visible. In between each milecastle, there would also have been two smaller turrets acting as watchtowers.

☆ North Pennines As you walk back to Cawfields, you will see the North Pennines to the south-west. These hills mark the northernmost end of the long line of hills often referred to as 'England's backbone'. The highest point is Cross Fell (2,920 feet) in Cumbria.

North Pennines | Turret 41A ☆ | ☆ Caw Gap | Milecastle 41 ☆ | 1¼ miles

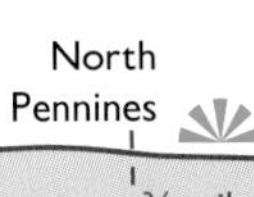

¾ mile | 5 Stile | 6 | 1 mile | 7 End of outward walk

2 ➡Beyond gates, head up to **left** on grass, very soon passing to right of Roman milecastle 42. Path not obvious at first.

3 ➡Path becomes clearer beyond milecastle climbing to Hadrian's Wall.
➡Continue along path with wall on left.

NATURE NOTES

Rowan, also known as mountain ash. In folklore it has associations with witchcraft and was planted to ward off evil spirits

The exposed rock in Cawfields Quarry is part of the Great Whin Sill, the same line of dolerite rock on which Bamburgh and Dunstanburgh castles are built. As you walk beside the wall, you'll see several hardy tree species, such as birch and rowan, clinging to the steep slopes on its northern side. In spring, listen for the evocative, high-pitched tremolo of the curlew, Britain's largest wading bird. Cattle and sheep, including Swaledales, graze the open grassland beside the wall.

Curlew

7 Start of return walk — Milecastle 41 — 1½ miles — Caw Gap — 6 — 5 Stile — Turret 41A — 1¾ miles — North Pennines

4 ➡After about 500 yards, wall and accompanying path drop into first of many dips.
➡Climb stone steps on other side and continue as before to reach a stile in 400 yards.

5 ➡Cross stile just before turret 41A at Caw Gap.
➡Keep forward to next kissing-gate.

Swaledale sheep

Birch

Great Whin Sill

Milecastle 42

Hadrian's Wall; National Trails

Crawfield Crags

Quarry pool

4 2 miles

2¼ miles

3 2 1

2½ miles

6 ➨Beyond kissing-gate, cross quiet lane and go through kissing-gate opposite.
➨Climb steep stone steps and walk on with the wall on left.

7 ➨On reaching gate in wall running perpendicular to Hadrian's Wall, don't go through it.
➨Instead, turn round and retrace steps to car park.

WALK 10 

RIVER TYNE AT HEXHAM

The historic market town of Hexham lies in the Tyne valley, just downstream from where the rivers North Tyne and South Tyne unite for their journey to the sea. This walk combines an exploration of the attractive town centre with a stroll through woods and along a riverside path. You'll get to see several interesting old buildings, including Hexham's medieval abbey and moot hall, and enjoy the tranquillity and the wildlife of the surrounding woodland and parks.

Distance
3.5 miles/5.6km

Time
1¾ hours

Start/Finish
Hexham

Parking NE46 3HQ
Tyne Green Country Park car park

Public toilets
Tyne Green Country Park

Cafés/pubs
Café Enna (Tynedale Golf Club); Hexham

Terrain
Pavement through town; shared-use surfaced paths; woodland; golf course; short section beside busy A road

Hilliness
Undulating with moderate climbs and descents; two long flights of steps either side of 6

Dogs
Dogs welcome but on leads. No stiles

Footwear
Winter
Spring/Autumn
Summer

Public transport
Train services operate on the Carlisle to Newcastle upon Tyne line, with railway station accessed between the walk start and 1. Hexham bus station is a short distance from 1

Accessibility
Mostly good path surfaces, except between 4 and 6. Some inclines might be difficult for self-propelled wheelchairs, and there are steps just before 3 and either side of 6.

Did you know? Hexham Bridge is a Grade II Listed structure built in 1793. It had two late 18th-century predecessors, the first built in 1770 and washed away by flooding the following year, and the second, crossing slightly further downstream, was opened in 1781 but only lasted until 1782. Before this crossing ferries operated between the north and south banks, and it is uncertain as to whether there were earlier bridges.

Local legend The still-heard expression 'Go to Hexham!' may have its origins in a Newcastle curse, possibly based on the fact that Hexham had the first purpose-built gaol (see page 77) in England.

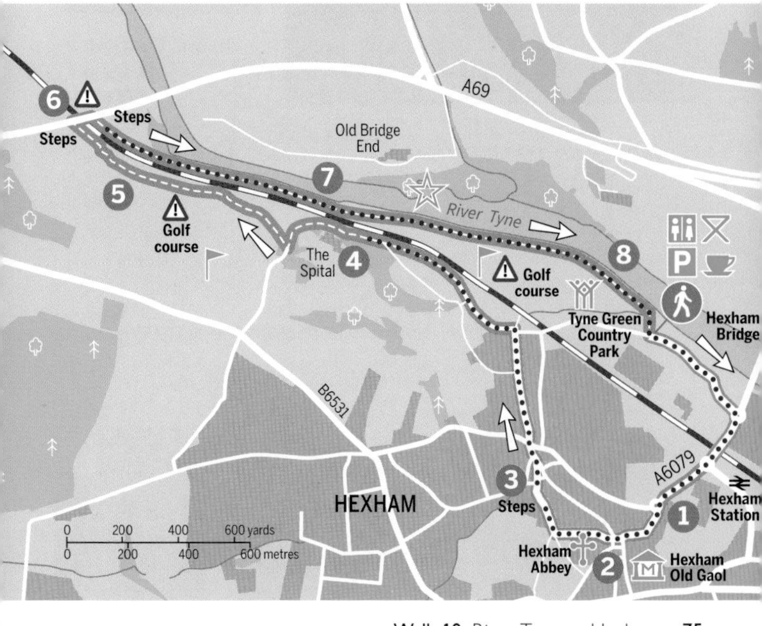

STORIES BEHIND THE WALK

Hexham Abbey St Wilfrid established a church on the site in the 7th century, although all that remains of the original stone building is the Saxon crypt. Most of the rest of the imposing, Gothic-style structure was built between 1170 and 1250. Among the medieval features still visible today are painted panels, a rood screen and various sculptures. The 'frith stool' or bishop's seat, made from a block of sandstone, probably dates from the 7th century.

Tyne Green Country Park
The walk ends with a stroll through Tyne Green Country Park. The industrialist and Liberal politician, Lord Allendale, presented this area to the people of Hexham in 1887 in celebration of Queen Victoria's golden jubilee. Avenues of trees were planted and public walkways laid out.

Hexham Old Goal

Hexham Abbey

Steps

½ mile

➡ From parking bays, walk back along Tyne Green Country Park's access lane.
➡ Turn **right** on pavement at roundabout on A6079. Go **straight over** next roundabout.

1 ➡ At third roundabout, take narrow lane (Hallstile Bank) climbing **left**.
➡ At top, go briefly **left** and then make directly for Hexham Abbey.

2 ➡ Take paved path to right of abbey. At junction of three lanes, turn **right**.
➡ At bottom of steep drop, descend steps on **right**. Go forward a few paces to Glovers Place.

Hexham Old Gaol

Using stone from the Roman town at nearby Corbridge, the gaol was built in 1333, making it England's first purpose-built prison. The building now houses a museum that contains exhibitions about the Reivers (criminal families that dominated the Anglo-Scottish border, see page 31) and about the grim reality of medieval crime and punishment.

☆ River Tyne

Hexham sits on the south side of the mighty River Tyne, which later flows through Newcastle and out into the North Sea. Its two main arms – the rivers North Tyne and South Tyne – meet less than one mile upstream of Tyne Green Country Park. While the North Tyne rises in the Kielder forests, the South Tyne comes racing down from the North Pennines.

1 mile

1½ miles

3 ➡Keep **straight ahead** at junction of residential streets and stay **left** at next junction. ➡Reaching busier road, go **straight over**. Towards end of road, turn **left** beside sports pitch. ➡Stay with lane for just under ½ mile. It eventually runs beside railway.

4 ➡Nearing white gate, take path heading uphill between black-and-white posts on **left**. ➡Gradient briefly eases. As path starts climbing again, turn **right** through wall gap. ➡Follow path skirting edge of golf course for 650 yards.

NATURE NOTES

Among the many tree species you'll see on this walk are common lime, planted beside the public paths in Tyne Green Country Park, and beech. As in so many towns around Britain, Hexham's public spaces spring back to life with the vibrant yellow of daffodils in March and April. Watch for small flocks of bullfinches in wooded areas. For a true wildlife spectacle, salmon can be spotted leaping up the weir beneath Hexham Bridge in October and November.

Lime tree, Tyne Green Country Park

Daffodil

Golf course

2 miles

5

6

Main road

5 ➨ Pass round side of redundant ladder stile to descend through woods.
➨ Steps then lead up to A69.

6 ➨ Turn **right**, crossing road bridge.
➨ Descend steps on far side and then turn **left** along shared-used path.
➨ Continue on path beside River Tyne (left) and railway (right) for ½ mile.

Male bullfinch

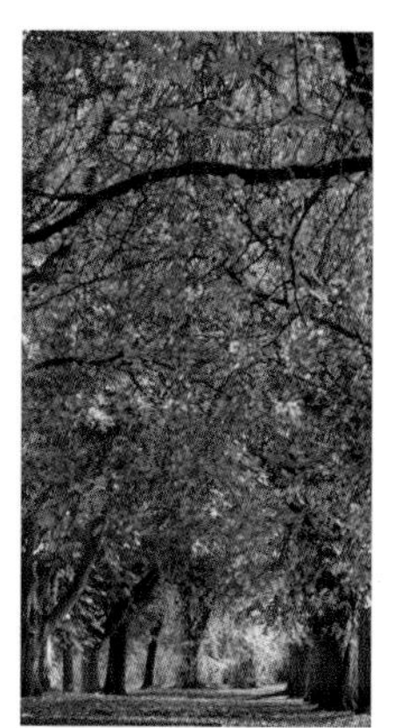
Beech avenue by River Tyne

Beech trees, Tyne Green Country Park. Beech is a magnificent native deciduous tree: it has a beautiful smooth grey bark and its leaves are a glorious first-flush green in spring turning to rich golden hues in autumn

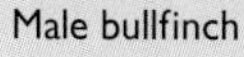

Tyne Green Country Park

River Tyne

3½ miles

Golf course

3 miles

7 ➡ Nearing white gate, bear **left** at fork in path.
➡ Entering Tyne Green Country Park, keep **left** along broad path near river for ¾ mile to Y-junction.

8 ➡ At fork, bear **right**, staying on tree-lined path. Cross small footbridge.
➡ Parking bays where walk started are on far side of children's play area.

Publishing information

ISBN 978 0 319092 30 9
1st edition published by Ordnance Survey 2022.

www.ordnancesurvey.co.uk

While every care has been taken to ensure the accuracy of the route directions, the publishers cannot accept responsibility for errors or omissions, or for changes in details given. The countryside is not static: hedges and fences can be removed, stiles can be replaced by gates, field boundaries can alter, footpaths can be rerouted and changes in ownership can result in the closure or diversion of some concessionary paths. Also, paths that are easy and pleasant for walking in fine conditions may become slippery, muddy and difficult in wet weather.

If you find an inaccuracy in either the text or maps, please contact Ordnance Survey at os.uk/contact.

A catalogue record for this book is available from the British Library.

Milestone Publishing credits

Author: Vivienne Crow

Series editor: Kevin Freeborn

Maps: Cosmographics

Design and Production: Patrick Dawson, Milestone Publishing

Printed in the Malta by Gutenberg Press

Photography credits

Front cover: Paulpixs/Shutterstock.com. **Back cover** cornfield/Shutterstock.com.

All photographs supplied by the author ©Vivienne Crow except pages 6 Ordnance Survey; 52 Kevin Freeborn; 67 Felicity Martin.

The following images were supplied by Shutterstock.com: page 1 Helen Hotson; 3 Dave Head; 18 Maciej Olszewski; 18 Maciej Olszewski; 19 oceanfishing; 19 Chanonry; 20 Dave Head; 24 Gallinago_media; 24 Michal Pesata; 25 Martin Fowler; 26 Henk Bogaard; 27 iLongLoveKing; 32 Karin Jaehne; 33 Holm94; 38 Agami Photo Agency; 39 Christoph Mischke; 39 David Osborn; 40 Krom1975; 40 SanderMeertinsPhotography; 41 Mark Heighes; 41 PJ photography; 41 Ondrej Prosicky; 41 Wang LiQiang; 46 WildMedia; 46 Mr James Woodhead; 47 Barry and Carole Bowden; 59 Adventuring Dave; 59 seawhisper; 60 Deborah Benbrook; 60 chrisdorney; 66 Voodison328; 67 Martin Fowler; 67 Nitr; 79 Piotr Krzeslak.